# Elephant vs. Rhinoceros

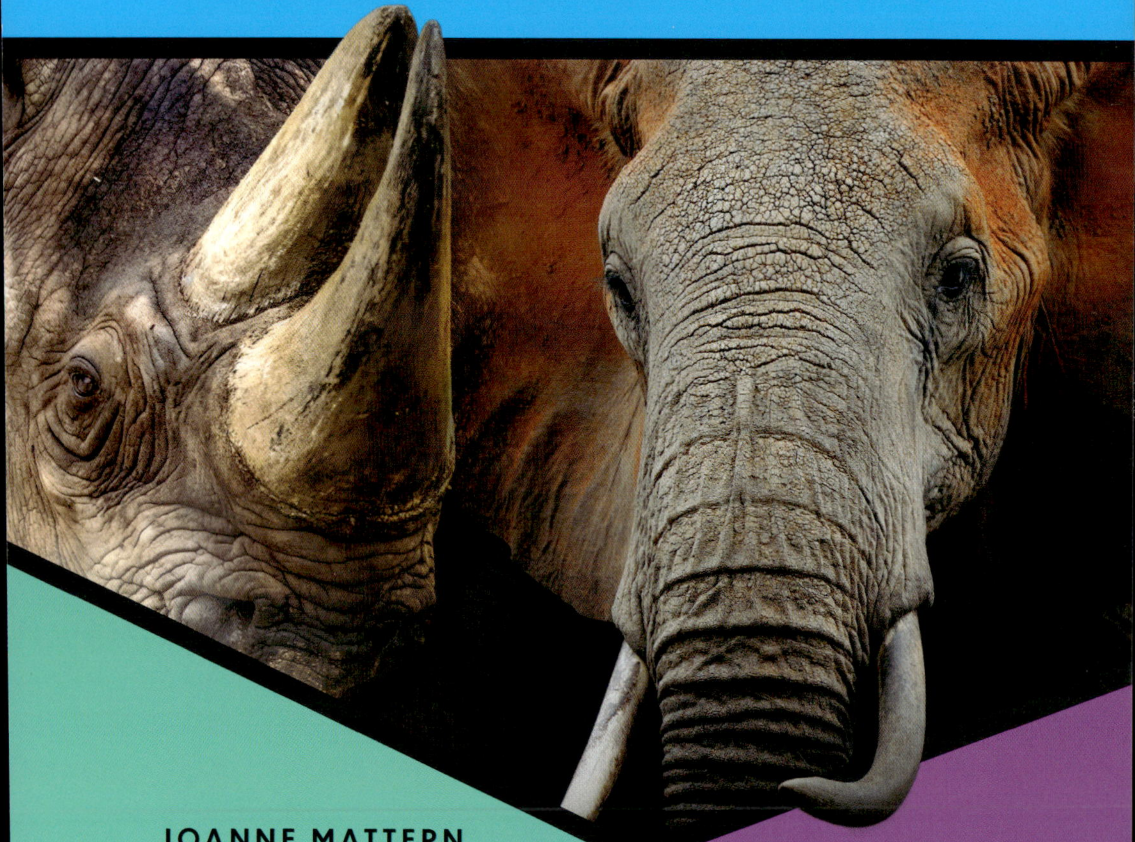

JOANNE MATTERN

Mitchell Lane
PUBLISHERS

## Parent and Caregiver Tips for Creating Nonfiction Readers

The high-interest topics in the *Nature's Rivals* series are sure to get your young reader excited about reading nonfiction. While exploring a fascinating subject, your reader will be introduced to new concepts, facts, ideas, and vocabulary.

## Tips for Reading Nonfiction

### Talk about Nonfiction

Explain that nonfiction books provide facts about real-world topics. When readers read nonfiction, they gain a rich understanding of the world. They build background knowledge that provides a foundation for learning and academic success.

### Look at the Parts

This book contains the following helpful features. Share the purpose of each feature with your reader.

***Photos, Captions, and Graphic Aids***
The photos, captions, charts, maps, and other graphic aids in nonfiction texts contain a wealth of information. Help your reader identify different ways information can be displayed.

***Sidebars***
These extra tidbits of information help satisfy readers' curiosity and expand their knowledge.

***Table of Contents***
Located at the front of the book, this list shows the big ideas within the text and the page numbers where they can be found.

***Glossary***
Located at the back of the book, the glossary defines key words and phrases that are related to the topic. These words and phrases can be found in the text in **bold** type.

***Comprehension Questions (Fact Check)***
Multiple-choice questions help readers self-check to make sure they understand what they read.

***Index***
Located at the back of the book, the index is an alphabetical list of topics and the page numbers where they can be found.

With a little help and guidance, your reader will be on their way to enjoying and learning from nonfiction books.

Mitchell Lane
PUBLISHERS
mitchelllanepub.com

2001 SW 31st Avenue
Hallandale, FL 33009



First Edition, 2026.
Author: Joanne Mattern
Designer: Jen Bowers
Editor: Tricia Hoffman

Series: Nature's Rivals
Title: Elephant vs. Rhinoceros / by Joanne Mattern

Hallandale, FL : Mitchell Lane Publishers, [2026]

Library bound ISBN: 979-8-89260-600-4
Paperback ISBN: 979-8-89260-612-7
eBook ISBN: 979-8-89260-609-7

PHOTO CREDITS
Alamy: Geir Olaf Gjerden, 3; Laura de Grasse, 23; Shutterstock: Ralph Lear, cover and 1, Volodymyr Burdiak, 1; imageBROKER.com, 4, COLOMBO NICOLA, 4; Papa Bravo, 5, 28; Triple Pines Studios, 6; Grobler du Preez, 7, Robin Hester, 7; Stu Porter, 8, 28; Stu Porter, 9, Zsolt Biczo, 9; Henk Bogaard, 10; MossStudio, 11, Ruwan Walpola, 11; kaskip, 12; meunierd, 13, Silarock, 13; THPStock, 14; kgo3121, 15; Johan Swanepoel, 16, Citra Novitasari Ziliwu, 16; JMx Images, 17; Nature Clickz, 18; NelisNienaber, 19; Lily Culham, 20; Jbrianne, 21; Grobler du Preez, 22, neelsky, 22; Roger de la Harpe, 23; zulfachri zulkifli, 24; Pearl Media, 25, Andrea Izzotti, 25; annabelle07, 26; EcoPrint, 27, PeopleImages.com, 27; Peter Hermes Furian, 28

# Contents

# Tusks vs. Horns

All is quiet on the African **savanna**. Many different **mammals** are looking for food. But food is hard to find for **herbivores** like the elephant. A **drought** means it hasn't rained in a long time, and there are not many plants to eat.

The elephant finds a tree that still has some tasty leaves. But a rhinoceros is already there, and he doesn't want to share! The rhino lowers his head and **charges** at the elephant. His sharp horn is pointed right at the elephant's head.

But the elephant doesn't back down. She uses her trunk to make a loud sound that means "back off!" When the rhino keeps coming, the elephant picks up some sticks in her trunk and throws them. But it's no use.

The rhino keeps coming. The elephant has no choice. She lowers her head and aims her two sharp **tusks** at the rhino. Then, she charges too. The battle is on! What will happen next?

# Enormous Elephants

African elephants are the largest land animals. Males stand almost 10 feet (3 meters) tall and weigh up to 13,228 pounds (6,000 kg). Even a **calf** can weigh 265 pounds (120 kg). That's more than most full-grown humans!

An elephant's huge size makes it a great fighter. This creature is bigger than any other animal that might attack it. An elephant can crush an enemy with the heavy weight of its body.

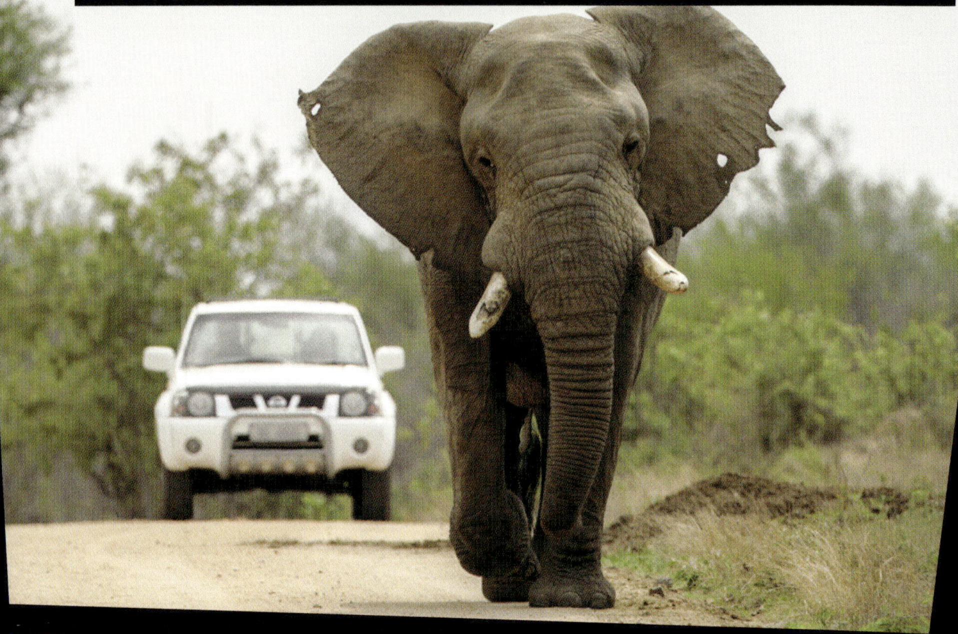

## Long Lives

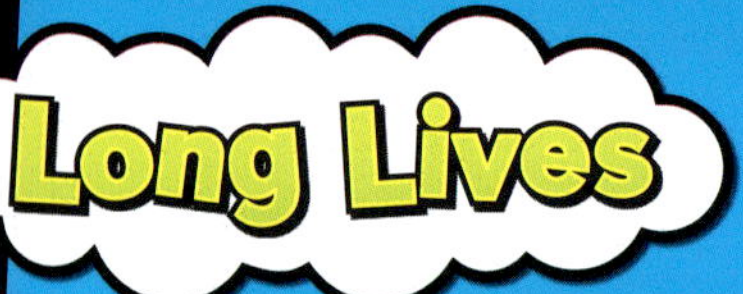

African elephants can live for 60 to 70 years.

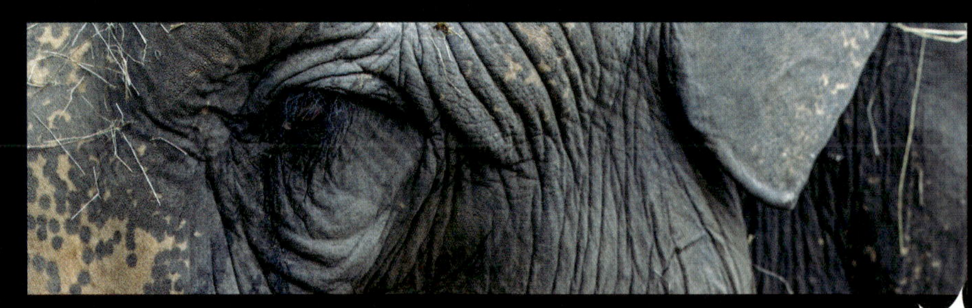

Elephants have two long top teeth, or tusks. One tusk can weigh more than 100 pounds (45 kg). These tusks can be up to eight feet (2.5 meters) long. Females have smaller tusks than males.

An elephant's tusk is a mighty weapon. An elephant can stab another animal with its tusks. Tusks are also used for digging, lifting, and carrying food.

## Poaching Problems

Many elephants have been killed for their tusks. This illegal hunting is called poaching.

Elephants don't eat meat. The only food they eat is plants. Elephants chow down on more than 330 pounds (149 kg) of **vegetation** each day. Grass, leaves, fruit, bushes, tree bark, and roots are their favorite foods. They also drink 25 to 50 gallons (100 to 200 liters) of water each day.

Finding so much food takes a lot of time. Elephants spend most of their day eating. They often travel from place to place to find enough to eat.

## Smelly Situation

One elephant can produce up to 220 pounds (100 kg) of poop per day.

# Raging Rhinos

You would not want to meet a rhinoceros in the wild. Why? These animals are often in a bad mood. Rhinos have short tempers. It's easy to make them angry. And an angry rhino is a dangerous rhino!

One reason rhinos are so grouchy is they can't see very well. Their poor eyesight means that they can't tell who or what is coming toward them. So, they might get nervous and charge at an **intruder** right away.

Elephants have tusks, but rhinoceroses have horns. Just one horn, to be exact. That horn is made of keratin. That's the same material your fingernails are made of.

A rhino's horn makes a great weapon. This animal uses its horn to defend itself. Males also use their horns to defend their **territory** from other males. Horns are also useful for digging or breaking branches.

## What's in a Name?

The word "rhinoceros" comes from ancient Greek words meaning "nose horn."

A rhino has very thick skin. Rhino skin can be up to two inches (5 cm) thick. Their skin is thicker than the skin of any other animal.

A rhino's thick skin protects it from attacks by other animals. Rhinos like to lie in the mud to protect their skin from sunburn and biting insects.

Like elephants, rhinos are herbivores. They only eat plants. Their mouth is shaped like a point, which helps them pull leaves and other plants into their mouths.

Rhinoceroses like to be alone. Male rhinos usually live by themselves. Females live with their calves. Sometimes adult females live together.

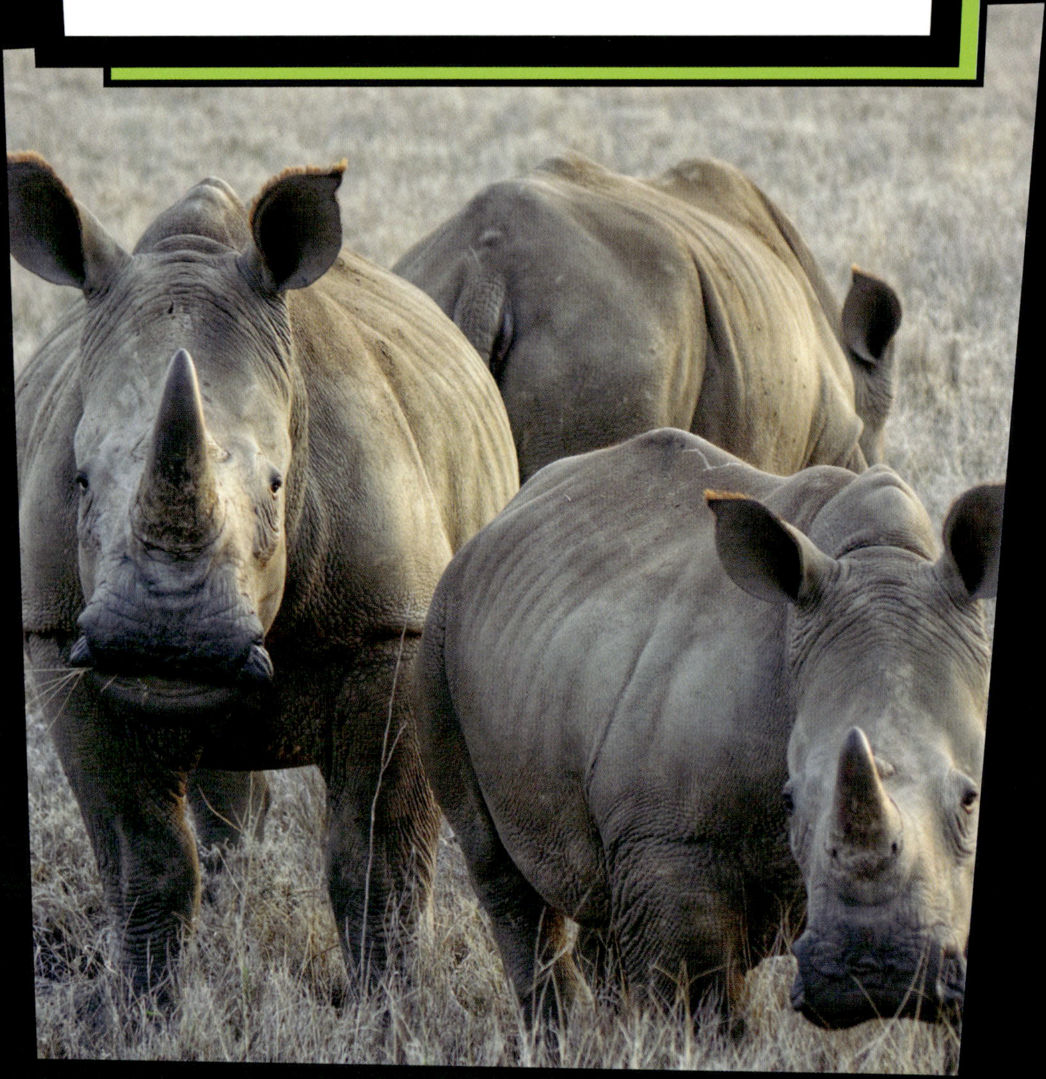

## Crash! Bang!

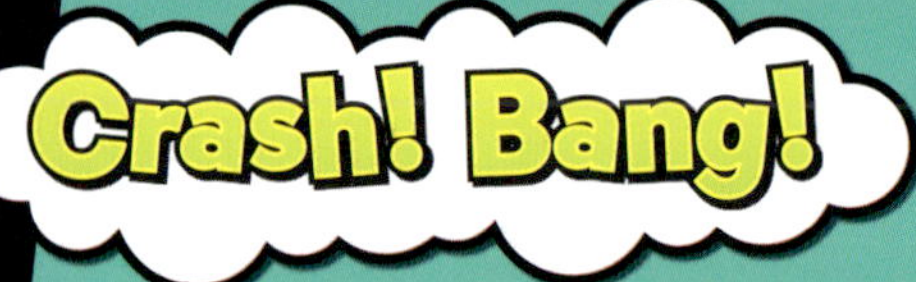

A group of rhinos is called a crash.

# A Fierce Battle

Our elephant and rhinoceros enemies are still fighting. The two animals were charging at each other the last time we saw them. What will happen next?

The rhino is a lot shorter than the elephant. He ducks under the elephant's head. Then, he drives his horn into the elephant's leg.

The elephant stumbles back. The rhino's horn has made a deep cut. Blood runs down the elephant's leg. But she is not about to give up.

The elephant lowers her head and runs forward. Her long tusks are pointed straight at the rhino. The sharp tusks strike the rhino's body.

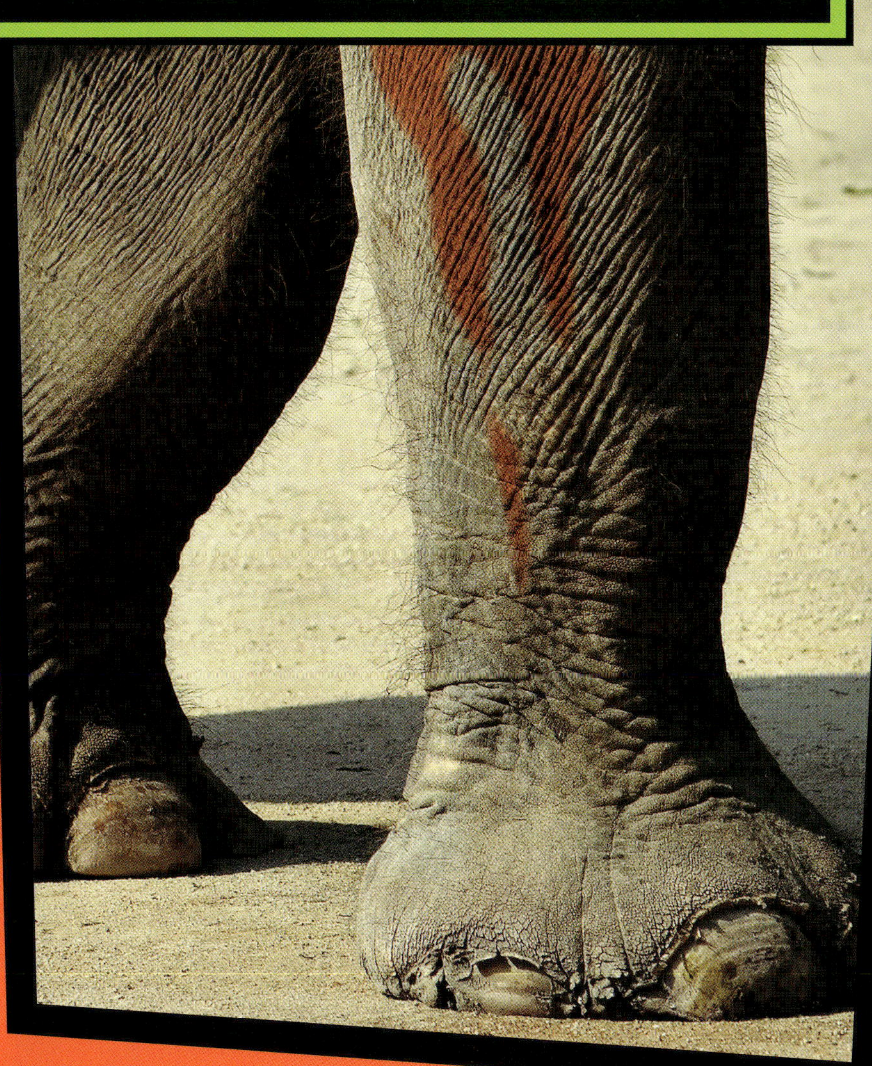

The rhino's thick skin protects him from serious injury. But the elephant isn't finished yet. She charges again, using her tusks to pick up the rhino. Then, she slams the rhino to the ground. If the elephant kneels on the rhino and crushes him, it will be all over.

What can the rhino do to protect himself? Think about each animal's weapons and defenses. Then, decide what you think will happen next in this deadly battle.

# Elephant vs. Rhinoceros

## Range of Elephant

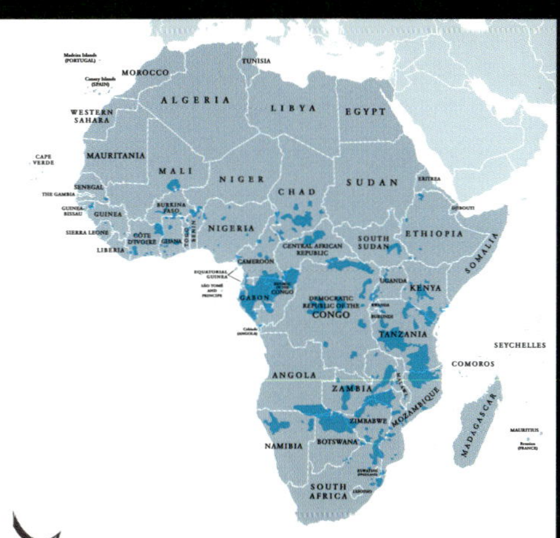


## Range of Rhinoceros

# Let's Compare

Elephant: Weight—up to 13,228 pounds (6,000 kg); Height—up to 10 feet (3 meters)

Rhino: Weight—More than 5,000 pounds (2,268 kg); Length—up to 6.5 feet (2 meters)

Elephant: 24 teeth and 2 tusks

Rhino: 24 to 34 teeth

Elephant: Long, sharp tusks, large size, heavy body

Rhino: Sharp horn

Elephant: Large size, heavy body

Rhino: Moves fast on land, heavy body, thick skin

# Glossary

**calf** (KAF)
a young elephant

**charges** (CHAHR-jez)
runs at something to attack

**drought** (DROUT)
a long period of weather without rain

**herbivores** (HUR-buh-vorz)
animals that only eat plants

**intruder** (in-TROO-der)
something that forces its way into a place

**mammals** (MAM-uhlz)
animals that are warm-blooded, have hair or fur, and nurse their babies

**savanna** (suh-VAN-uh)
a flat, grassy plain with few or no trees

**territory** (TER-i-tor-ee)
the area where an animal lives

**tusks** (TUHSKS)
long, curved, pointed teeth that stick out of an elephant's mouth

**vegetation** (vej-i-TAY-shuhn)
plants

1. Elephants and rhinos both eat ________.
   A. other animals  B. plants  C. both plants and animals

2. An elephant is the largest animal ________.
   A. on Earth  B. in water  C. on land

3. Rhinos have trouble ________.
   A. running  B. hearing  C. seeing

4. A rhino's ________ protects it from harm.
   A. thick skin  B. long horn  C. pointed mouth

Answers
1. B, 2. C, 3. C, 4. A

**BOOKS**

Adamson, Thomas K. *Rhinoceros vs. African Elephant.* Bellwether Media, 2020.

Barth, Kelley. *A Crash of Rhinos.* Child's World, 2024.

Gish, Melissa. *Elephants.* Creative Paperbacks, 2024.

Klepinger, Teresa. *Elephant vs. Rhino.* Kaleidoscope, 2022.

**ON THE INTERNET**

National Geographic Kids: 10 Unforgettable Elephant Facts!
www.natgeokids.com/uk/discover/animals/general-animals/elephant-facts/
Did you know these 10 amazing facts about elephants?

National Geographic Kids: Rhino Facts!
www.natgeokids.com/uk/discover/animals/general-animals/rhinoceros-facts/
Explore lots of interesting facts about rhinos.

## About the Author

Joanne Mattern has written many nonfiction books for children. She adores animals of all kinds. Although she's never seen a battle between an elephant and a rhinoceros, she enjoys visiting both animals in zoos, as well as reading and writing about them. Joanne lives in New York State with her family. Although there are no elephants or rhinoceroses there now, her father used to tell her stories about a neighbor who actually kept a small herd of elephants on his property a long time ago.

I0823262